SOPHIE LEARNS
SPANISH

Illustrated by Annabel Tempest
Written by Sue Finnie & Libby Mitchell

D1080413

ticktock
MEDIA

Copyright © **ticktock** Entertainment Ltd. 2003
Unit 2, Orchard Business Centre, North Farm Road, Tunbridge Wells, TN2 3XF.
First published in Great Britain in 2003 by **ticktock** Media Ltd.,
Text by Sue Finnie and Libby Mitchell
Illustrations by Annabel Tempest 2002
ISBN 1-86007-315-8
Printed in China
A CIP catalogue record for this book is available from the British Library.

¡Hola!

Welcome to Spain. Join our visit to this amazing country, and learn the basics of the Spanish language along the way.

Read

1

Follow Sophie and Pablo's adventures in Spain as they take part in a fiesta, watch a football match and much more.

Learn

2

All the Spanish words in this book are in **bold.** If you want to find out what they mean, turn to the handy phrasebook on each spread. There is also an easy-to-follow guide to pronunciation to help you speak Spanish.

Listen

3

The CD-Rom completes the experience. Each screen you see is identical to the pages in the book, so you can hear the spoken Spanish. There are four great games too. Load up the disk and have fun!

LLEGADAS ▶▶

SERVICIOS ◀◀

EQUIPAJE ◀◀

INFORMACIÓN ▶▶

After a very long plane ride, Sophie has finally arrived in Spain. She is going to stay for a week with her cousin Pablo and his family. She's never met them before. How will she get along?

Este es mi hermano. Se llama Juan.

Esta es mi abuelita. Se llama María.

Este es mi padre. Se llama Manuel.

Hola. Me llamo Sophie.

Hola. Me llamo Pablo.

Esta es mi madre. Se llama Violeta.

Este es mi perro. Se llama Curro.

Sophie

Pablo says hello: **"¡Hola! Me llamo Pablo."** He asks if Sophie speaks Spanish. **"¿Hablas español?"** **"Sí, hablo español"** she replies. Luckily, she speaks a bit of Spanish and she has her little phrasebook. (It will be useful for you too!)

Outside the airport, Sophie points at the sun.
"¡Hace calor!" Yes, it is hot. Sophie and
Pablo both like hot weather. But it's TOO hot
for Curro with his warm
coat. Poor Curro!

Sophie's Phrasebook

el taxi

TAXI

TAXI

la carretera

"¿De dónde eres?"
The taxi driver is asking
Sophie where she comes from.
"Soy de California" she smiles.

Say your
name in
Spanish.

Me llamo...

"Esta es mi casa." This is Pablo's house. Curro finds a great way to cool down while Pablo welcomes Sophie to his home: **"Mi casa es tu casa."** He's telling her to make herself at home.

Sophie's Phrasebook

el salón

la lámpara

el sofá

el sillón

la alfombra

la piscina

In the garden and on the terrace, there are lots of colourful plants and flowers. Pablo asks Sophie if she likes flowers: *"¿Te gustan las flores?"* Sophie nods yes: *"¡Sí!"* She loves flowers: *"¡Me gustan las flores!"*

Where is Curro the dog?

Está en...

la cocina

la cocina

las flores

el fregadero

la mesa

el comedor

las plantas

la silla

la terraza

"¿Dónde está Juan?" asks Pablo. Where is Juan?
Sophie spots the naughty toddler: *"Está en el salón!"*
Juan is emptying a plant pot all over the living-room floor.
Pablo shouts out to him: *"¡Juan, ven aquí!"*

Este es el dormitorio. Pablo's bedroom is full of really interesting things. He's a big football fan and very proud of his collection of football shirts. Sophie counts them with him: *"Uno, dos, tres, cuatro, cinco, seis, siete, ocho, nueve, diez."*

un oso de peluche

un balón

una ventana

un tejado

un armario

uno

dos

un libro

seis

tres

cuatro

cinco

siete   ocho   nueve

Ten soccer shirts! Juan has a look in the wardrobe, just to check if there are any more. But he can't find any and shakes his head: *"¡No!"*

Pablo [...]
He explo[...]
póster, [...]
around t[...]
"¿Tien[...]
doesn't [...]

Este es... (ess-tay ess)	This is...
el dormitorio (el dor-me-tor-ee-o)	the bedroom
¿Tienes...? (tee-en-es)	Have you got...?
Tengo... (teng-go)	I've got...
¡Mira! (mee-ra)	Look!
uno (oo-no)	one
dos (doss)	two
tres (tress)	three
cuatro (qua-troe)	four
cinco (thing-ko)	five
seis (say-ss)	six
siete (see-yete)	seven
ocho (o-choe)	eight
nueve (nwe-vay)	nine
diez (dee-eth)	ten

un oso de peluche (oon osso day pell-oo-che)	a teddy bear
un balón (oon bal-on)	a ball
un armario (oon ar-mar-ee-o)	a wardrobe
un libro (oon lee-bro)	a book
un tejado (oon te-har-doe)	a roof
una ventana (oona ven-tar-na)	a window
una cama (oona kama)	a bed
una almohada (oona al-mo-ahr-da)	a pillow
un reloj (oon ray-lo)	a clock
un pupitre (oon poo-pee-tray)	a desk
una silla (oona see-ya)	a chair
una radio (oona rad-ee-o)	a radio
un Gameboy (oon Gameboy)	a Gameboy
un póster (oon post-air)	a poster
un televisor (oon tel-e-vee-saw)	a tv

un póster

una almohada

un pupitre

un reloj

diez

un Gameboy

una cama

una silla

una radio

Say what you've got in your room.

Tengo...

Then Sophie spots something strange…
an enormous pillow! She tells Pablo to look:
"¡Mira!" Pablo laughs: it's just Curro
playing hide-and-seek under the pillow.

Where in the town would you go to...
a) see a boat?
b) catch a train?
c) see a film?

You can see lots of places from the balcony. Pablo points out some places to Sophie: *"Mira, Sophie. El puerto, la iglesia, la plaza y las casas."* Little Juan can see mountains in the distance. *"¡Las montañas, las montañas!"* he calls.

las montañas

la pescadería

el parque

la librería

el autobús

el tren

la

el balcón

la moto

la panadería

la bicicleta

la plaza

"Tengo hambre." Sophie is really hungry as it's much later than she usually eats. Her aunt offers her some chicken with rice: *"¿Quieres pollo con arroz, Sophie?"* Sophie nods: *"¡Sí, por favor!"* She tells them all it's delicious: *"¡Está rico!"* Now Sophie is thirsty. *"Tengo sed."* Pablo offers her some lemonade. *"¿Quieres limonada?"* Yes please! she replies. *"¡Sí, por favor!"*

el plato

el pollo

el pan

las zanahorias

el tenedor

el jamón

la ensalada

el cuchillo

las judías verdes

la limonada

el queso

el pescado

el arroz

la cuchara

el plátano

los pasteles

When her aunt offers her more Sophie's so full she has to say no: *"¡No, gracias!"* Juan wants another banana though: *"¡Quiero un plátano!"* Everybody starts laughing.

After lunch, Grandma yawns and says she's tired: **_"Tengo sueño."_** It's siesta time and everyone has a rest or a nap, including the dog. Pablo explains that they often stay indoors and rest for a while after lunch as it's too hot to go outside.

Say what you want to eat or drink.

Quiero...

Sophie's Phrasebook

Sophie thinks it's unusual, but she soon nods off after her long journey and her huge lunch, even though Grandma and Curro are both snoring like growling lions!

Sophie's Phrasebook

Later on it's the evening paseo. Everyone comes out to walk about and meet and chat with their friends. Her aunt and uncle greet everybody they know, saying: **"¡Buenas tardes!"**

LA TIENDA DE DISCOS

la joyería

LA TIENDA DE REGALOS

los caramelos

las flores

los animales

los pájaros

Sophie is fascinated by all the stalls and street entertainers. She wants to buy a songbird but her aunt persuades her to buy candy – **caramelos** – instead.

Juan starts to cry when his balloon flies away into the night sky. He cheers up a bit when he sees Curro trying to help the juggler. Everyone shouts: **"¡Bravo!"** – what a clever dog!

Point to the different parts of your face and say what they are called in Spanish.

el pelo   los ojos
la nariz
las orejas
la boca

An artist draws a cartoon picture of Sophie and asks her if she likes it:
"¿Te gusta?"
Sophie thinks it's funny:
"Es divertido!"

The follow...
Sophie if sh...
beach: "¿Qu...
"¡Sí, claro!...
delight. She ...

¿Quieres ir a la playa? (key-air-ess i-rr a la pl-eye-ya)	Would you like to go to the beach?
¿Quieres ir a...? (key-air-ess i-rr a)	Would you like to go...
¡Sí, claro! (see, klar-roe)	Yes, of course.
La playa es preciosa (la pl-eye-ya ess pre-thi-os-sa)	The beach is beautiful
...es preciosa (ess pre-thi-os-sa)	...is beautiful
¿Te gusta...? (tay goos-ta)	Do you like...?
Me gusta... (may goos-ta)	I like...
Sí, me gusta (see, may goos-ta)	Yes, I like (it)
No, no me gusta (no no may goos-ta)	No, I don't like (it)
pero (pair-ro)	but
Juguemos (hu-ga-moss)	Let's play
el traje de baño (el tr--hay day ban-yo)	swimsuit

la toalla (la toe-al-ya)	towel
las gafas de sol (las ga-fass)	sunglasses
el sombrero (el som-brair-ro)	hat
la camiseta (la ka-me-se-ta)	t-shirt
los pantalones cortos (los pant-a-lon-ess cor-tos)	shorts
las sandalias (las san-dal-lee-ass)	sandals
la crema solar (la kre-ma so-lar)	suncream
el fútbol (el foot-bol)	football
el voleibol (el vo-lay-bol)	volleyball
el béisbol (el base-bol)	baseball
la pesca (la pes-ka)	fishing
la vela (la ve-la)	sailing
el windsurf (el windsurf)	windsurfing
la natación (la nat-a-thion)	swimming

la vela

la natación

el windsurf

el sombrero

las gafas de sol

la camiseta

la toalla

los pantalones cortos

las sandalias

el traje de baño

The sand is white and the sea is clear and turquoise blue. It's the most beautiful beach Sophie has ever seen. *"La playa es preciosa,"* she says to Pablo. *"¡Juguemos!"* Pablo is delighted to have a friend to play with on the beach. *"¿Te gusta el fútbol? ¿Te gusta el béisbol?"* he asks Sophie. *"Sí, me gusta el fútbol y me gusta el béisbol...pero no me gusta la pesca."* She likes football and baseball but she doesn't like fishing.

el voleibol

el béisbol

el fútbol

Look at the beach and say what you like doing.

Me gusta...

la crema solar

The next day, Pablo takes Sophie to meet the animals at Tío Antonio´s ranch. *"Buenos días, Tío Antonio,"* Pablo calls to his uncle. *"¡Hola, Pablo! ¡Hola, Sophie!"* he replies, smiling. Pablo can imitate the animals´ noises. *"Mu mu, bee bee, cuac cuac, pío pío."* Sophie laughs so much that Curro starts barking: *"¡Guau, guau, guau!"*

la oveja

el caballo

la vaca

el perro

el toro

Cuidado!

el cerdo

Pablo says **"Cuídado, Sophie. El toro es peligroso."** But Sophie isn't worried about the fierce bull. **"Me gusta el pollito."** She likes the chick. **"Es muy simpático."** It's very friendly.

Sophie's Phrasebook

el gato

el pato

la gallina

el pollito

Say which animals you like.

Me gusta...

Today is an important day – there is a fiesta in the town. Sophie and Pablo are wearing special clothes. There are games and singing and dancing. Pablo asks Sophie to dance: **"¿Quieres bailar?"**

verde

púrpura

rojo

amarillo

Sophie's Phrasebook

la chaqueta

los pantalones

los calcetines

el vestido

los zapatos

There are even fireworks to watch. *"¿Cuál es tu color favorito?"* asks Pablo. *"Mi color favorito es azul"* says Sophie. She likes blue best. Pablo prefers the red firework. *"Mi color favorito es el rojo."*

blanco

azul

What's your favourite colour?

Mi color favorito es

el poncho

el sombrero

la blusa

la falda

la camisa

una piña

un plátano

una manzana

una naranja

un limón

una sandía

una papaya

un coco

un melón

Pablo and Sophie are buying some fruit at the market. Sophie loves the colours of all the different fruit. The pineapples and oranges look delicious and very juicy. The papayas are huge! But in the end Sophie asks for a melon. *"Un melón, por favor."* Pablo wants a pineapple: *"Una piña, por favor."*

"¿Quieres un helado, Sophie?" asks Pablo, pointing at the ice cream shop. Sophie says that's a good idea: **"¡Buena idea!"** She can remember some of the names of the fruit to help her choose her ice cream: **"Un helado de fresa, limón y mango, por favor."** Pablo looks at the other flavours on the ice-cream board and asks for **"Chocolate, vainilla y fresa."**

Ask for the ice cream you would like.

Un helado de...

La de Micho

piña
limón
naranja
coco
fresa
chocolate
café
vainilla

un helado

On Friday there's a big soccer match in the stadium. It's Pablo's birthday, and for a special treat the family are going to see the big game. *"¡Feliz cumpleaños!"* says Sophie. *"¿Cuántos años tienes?"* She's asking how old he is. *"Tengo ocho años."* Pablo is eight years old!

Sophie is amazed at the size of the stadium. **"El estadio es muy grande,"** she says. **"Sí, es enorme,"** replies Pablo. Then Sophie looks at ... **muy pe...**

Spanish	Pronunciation	English
Feliz cumpleaños	(fe-lith kum-play-an-yos)	Happy Birthday
¿Cuántos años tienes?	(quan-tos an-yos tée-en-ess)	How old are you?
Tengo ocho años	(ten-go o-choe an-yos)	I'm eight years old
Tengo...años	(ten-go...an-yos)	I'm... years old
El estadio es muy grande	(el ess-tard-thee-o ess mwee gran-day)	The stadium is very big
Juan es muy pequeño	(hwuarn ess mwee pe-ken-yo)	Juan is very small
...es muy grande	(ess mwee gran-day)	...is very big
...es muy pequeño	(ess mwee pe-ken-yo)	...is very small
Si, es enorme	(see, es e-nor-may)	Yes, it's enormous

Spanish	Pronunciation	English
grande	(gran-day)	big
enorme	(e-nor-may)	enormous
pequeño	(pe-ken-yo)	small
alto	(al-toe)	tall
bajo	(ba-ho)	short
el balón	(el ba-lon)	the ball
el equipo	(el eki-po)	the team
el árbitro	(el ar-bee-tro)	the referee
el portero	(el por-tair-o)	goalkeeper
el delantero	(el dea-lan-tair-o)	forward/striker
el gol	(el gol)	goal
los espectadores	(los es-pek-ta-dor-ess)	the crowd

los espectadores

BOL

el árbitro

el delantero

el balón

What is grande and who is pequeño?

La tienda de regalos

el juego

el póster

el abanico

la tarjeta postal

el balón

la camiseta

el llavero

la pluma

el libro

la muñeca

It's the last day of Sophie's holiday. She wants to buy some presents to take home. She chooses dolls for her Mom and Dad, and something for Pablo and Juan too. As she has a little bit of money left, Sophie wants to know how much the fan is. **"¿Cuánto es el abanico?"** she asks. It costs six euros. She decides to buy one. **"Un abanico, por favor,"** Sophie asks the shopkeeper

Sophie says goodbye to everyone. *"Adiós, Pablo. Adiós, Juan. Adiós, Curro."* They are all so sad to see her go but they hope she´ll come back soon. *"Adiós, Sophie. ¡Hasta pronto!"*

Sophie's Phrasebook

"Adiós, Pablo. Adiós, Juan. Adiós, Curro!"

My Spanish Holiday Scapbook

Pablo lives here

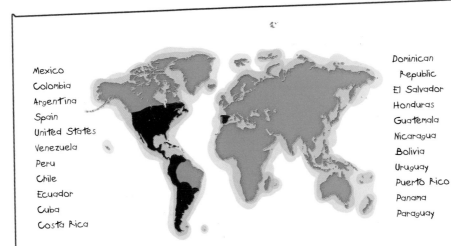

Mexico
Colombia
Argentina
Spain
United States
Venezuela
Peru
Chile
Ecuador
Cuba
Costa Rica

Dominican
 Republic
El Salvador
Honduras
Guatemala
Nicaragua
Bolivia
Uruguay
Puerto Rico
Panama
Paraguay

The shaded areas on the map show where Spanish is spoken in the world.